IT WAS LIKE A DREAM

"HOLDING ON TO GOD WHEN EVERYTHING SAYS LET GO"

———————————

REV. MRS. NAOMI ANTWI

IT WAS LIKE A DREAM
Copyright © 2025 by Rev. Mrs. Naomi Antwi

Printed in the USA
Cover Designed by Naadkwam.com

For information contact:

Website: www.naomiantwi.com

Email: revnantwi@gmail.com

*"When the Lord brought back his exiles to Jerusalem, **it was like a dream**!*

We were filled with laughter, and we sang for joy. And the other nations said,

"What amazing things the Lord has done for them."

~ Psalm 126:1-2 NLT ~

DEDICATION

This book is dedicated to my beloved husband, whose strength and love remain my anchor, and to our bright and beautiful children, whose wisdom and laughter light my path. It is also for everyone who has wept in silence, prayed through long nights, and waited with hope for a breakthrough that seemed beyond reach.

May these words remind you that God never forgets His children, and His promises bloom in perfect time.

TABLE OF CONTENTS

Foreword 9

Preface 13

Introduction 15

ACKNOWLEDGEMENTS 17

Chapter One 19

Chapter TWO 29

Chapter THREE 37

Chapter FOUR 47

Chapter FIVE 59

Chapter SIX 67

Chapter SEVEN 73

Chapter EIGHT 81

Chapter NINE 99

Chapter TEN 107

Chapter ELEVEN 115

Chapter TWELVE 127

EPILOGUE 133

APPENDIX 139

AUTHOR'S NOTE 170

ABOUT THE AUTHOR 172

A CALL TO ACTION 177

FOREWORD

There are some stories that are not simply told; they are lived, endured, and carried through valleys that most people never imagine they could survive. This is one of those stories. In these pages, you will walk with me through years of waiting, praying, fasting, and wrestling with God. You will see the raw pain of unanswered prayers, the crushing weight of despair, and the haunting temptation to give up completely.

Yet, you will also witness the faithfulness of God who never abandons His children, even when silence seems louder than His promises. This testimony is not polished to hide the tears or the questions. Instead, it lays bare the journey of faith when hope seemed lost.

It reveals how God speaks in the darkest nights, how He confirms His word, and how He strengthens His people to endure trials that feel unbearable. It is a reminder that the Christian walk is not always easy, but it is always purposeful. As you read, may you find yourself in these words. If you have ever prayed for years without seeing an answer, if you have ever wondered if God hears you, if you have ever been pressed to the point of breaking, this story is for you. My journey will remind you that God is never late, never silent without reason, and never unfaithful to His promises.

He is the same God who parted the Red Sea, strengthened Gideon, answered Daniel, made Esther Queen, and who still holds His children with His victorious right hand today.
This book is not just a testimony - it is an invitation.

An invitation to trust, to persevere, and to discover for yourself that God truly writes the most powerful stories when we are at the end of ourselves. May your faith be renewed, your hope restored, and your spirit lifted as you turn each page.

Welcome to my journey.

- Rev. Mrs. Naomi Antwi -

PREFACE

When I first began this journey, I never imagined it would one day become a story to be shared with others. For years, my struggles were private, carried in silence between me and God.
I prayed, fasted, cried, and wrestled with questions that pierced my soul. I often wondered why God delayed, why He seemed silent, and why the answers I longed for never came when I expected them.

In time, I came to realize that my journey was not only about the fulfillment of a need, but also about the transformation of my heart. God was shaping me, even in the silence. He was teaching me endurance, humility, faith, and dependence on Him in ways I could not have learned otherwise.
What once felt like punishment, I now see as preparation.

This book is not written to glorify my pain, but to magnify the faithfulness of God who met me in my darkest hours.

It is my hope that as you read, you will not only walk with me through my story, but you will also see your own struggles in a new light.

If you are waiting for an answer from God, if you feel as though God has forgotten you, or if you have wrestled with despair, I want you to know that you are not alone.

The same God who strengthened me will strengthen you. The same God who upheld me with His victorious right hand will uphold you.

This testimony is my offering to the Lord and my gift to you.

May it bring encouragement, hope, and a reminder that even in the silence, God is working out His promises.

- *Rev. Mrs. Naomi Antwi -*

INTRODUCTION

Beloved, I want to speak to you heart-to-heart. Life can be hard - sometimes unbearably so. There are days when hope feels distant, when prayers feel unanswered, and when the weight of our struggles seems impossible to carry. I have been there. I have felt broken, lost, and utterly unsure of what comes next.

"It Was Like a Dream" is the journey of my brokenness, my perseverance, my prayers and fasts, my moments of despair, and ultimately, my experience of God's unshakable grace. But it's not just my story. It is a testament to the truth that God's promises never fail, His miracles still exists, His timing is always perfect, and His ways are far beyond what we could ever imagine,

think, or dream. As you read these pages, know that you are not alone.

If you are searching for hope, holding onto faith, or simply wondering if God sees you, this book is for you.

May my journey remind you that even in the darkest valleys, God's light is closer to you than you think and His love will never run out on you.

ACKNOWLEDGEMENTS

I am profoundly grateful to everyone who has walked with me on this journey.

To my husband, my children, and my family – your steadfast love, prayers, and encouragement have been my anchor in moments of weariness.

To my friends and colleagues who reminded me of God's promises when hope felt distant - thank you for lifting me up.

To my mentors and spiritual guides - your wisdom, guidance, and gentle nudges to press on have shaped the pages of this book; it carries your fingerprints.

And to every believer who has ever shared a word, a song, or a scripture that brightened my darkest days - this story is as much yours as it is mine.

Above all, I give thanks to God, who did not allow shame or disgrace to claim me, but turned my mourning into joyful dancing. Truly, He has placed a song of praise in my heart, one I now share with the world.

CHAPTER ONE

DESPERATE NEED

Many people walk through life with smiles on their faces, giving the impression that all is well. But behind those smiles, there is often silent pain, unspoken struggles, and hidden battles that no one else sees. I know, because I was one of them.

On the outside, I looked fine. I laughed. I showed up. I kept going. But deep inside, there was turmoil I couldn't put into words. I was carrying a load far too heavy for me to handle. Day after day, I asked God for strength, even when it felt like my prayers were barely reaching His ears. There comes a point in life when human solutions run out. I reached that point. I was desperate and crushed inside.

For years, I carried a need so heavy that it threatened to crush me. It wasn't something money could fix. It wasn't something friends could solve even if they wanted to. It wasn't even something my husband could fully carry with me. It was life or death. And the only One I could turn to was God. I prayed. Oh, how I prayed.

I called on the name of the Lord morning, afternoon, evening, and night.

At first, I prayed with confidence, believing that within days, my situation would change for the better. But days became weeks, weeks became months, and months stretched into years. Still, there was no answer.

My prayers grew desperate. I grew more and more despondent.

I often thought of the Israelites at the edge of the Red Sea. Pharaoh's army thundered close behind them, dust rising from hundreds of chariots and horses.

In front of them, a sea stretched wide with no bridge, no ship, no boat, no way forward. It was a perfect trap for the people of God. That's where I lived - in that impossible place where every option is closed off, and only a miracle can save you.

I began to plead with God as Moses pleaded when the Israelites stood before that Red Sea. Except for me, there was no Moses lifting up his staff, raising his hand over the sea, and parting the sea. It was complete silence from Heaven.

Philippians 4:6 says, "*Don't worry about anything; instead, pray about everything. Tell God what you need, and thank Him for all He has done.*" (NLT)

I continued to do exactly that. I continued to pray, pray, and pray. Yet nothing seemed to change. Even when I wanted to give up, I couldn't, because I knew that if God didn't move, I would not survive. Either God made a way, or I was finished. It was as simple as that. People around me didn't know the depth of my struggle.

I smiled when I had to. I went about my duties as a mother, a wife, a sister, a daughter, a friend, and a Pastor.

But deep inside, I was broken. Every night, I fell to my knees, sometimes too weary to form words, only able to whisper, "Lord, please help me."

The word of God became my lifeline.

I clung to scriptures like Psalm 34:17, "*The Lord hears his people when they call to him for help. He rescues them from all their troubles.*" (NLT).

I read it again and again and again, trying to convince myself that God still heard me, even though the heavens felt silent.

The silence was the hardest part.

When you're desperate, every day without an answer feels like a lifetime.

I started to ask questions I never thought I would: "Does God exist?"

"Can He hear me?"

"Is He able to feel my pain?"

Psalm 56:8 states, "*You keep track of all my sorrows. You have collected all my tears in your bottle. You have recorded each one in your book.*" (NLT)

So, based on this scripture and God's silence, I asked myself, "Does God see my tears?"

"Was God ignoring me?"

"Did I do something wrong that He can't forgive?

"Did He even care?"

"What's the point?"

That desperate need - the one that made me feel like my entire life was hanging in the balance, like I was walking on thin ice, was the beginning of my journey.

Looking back now, I realize that God allowed me to come to the end of myself, so I would learn to fully depend on Him. But at that time, all I knew was hunger.

Hunger for signs and wonders, hunger for deliverance, hunger for God to show up, Hunger for miracles and breakthroughs. And so, I kept praying.

The years dragged on, and my need remained. Each time I prayed, I expected a shift, or a sign of God's favor, even a small one. But nothing moved.

Nothing changed. Nothing happened.

At some point, I began feeling like I was losing my mind because I kept doing the same thing - praying over and over, yet I expected a different outcome.

I knew God was able. I knew He could fix everything with a snap of His finger.

But He didn't.

I had read about His mighty works and power in Scripture. I had even experienced His goodness and faithfulness in the past. But in this matter, upon which my very life depended, it seemed as though the gates of heaven were closed to me and my prayers were unable to penetrate.

There is a special kind of pain that comes not when God says "No," but when He says nothing at all. I cried and prayed until I had no tears left. I pleaded until my words ran dry. At night I lay awake, staring at the ceiling, wondering if my prayers even reached God's ears.

In the quiet, dark hours of the night, doubt and fears whispered louder than my faith.

"Maybe God doesn't want to answer you."

"Maybe you've prayed wrong."

"Maybe He doesn't love you enough."

"Maybe He doesn't care about you".

"Maybe this is your fate, accept it"

The silence was deafening. Still, I couldn't stop praying. The habit of prayer was burned so deep into me that even in my despair I kept on praying. I prayed every day, every week, every year. I prayed multiple times per day. Even when I felt it was useless, I prayed. But inside, something was breaking. The weight of unanswered prayers pressed me down. It was in this heavy silence, when prayer felt pointless and God seemed so far away, that God began to prepare me for the next stage of my journey.

Discussion Questions:

1. Have you ever faced a situation that seemed impossible to overcome?
2. How did you respond when it seemed like God was silent?

Reflection Exercise:

1. Write down one situation in your life that feels like the Red Sea - impossible to cross.
2. Write a prayer of trust, asking God to make a way.

Prayer:

Dear Lord, please teach me to keep praying even when the answers seem delayed. Help me to trust your plan even when I cannot see it. Amen.

CHAPTER TWO

ADD FASTING

As the years stretched on, my prayers felt unanswered. I wondered if perhaps I was missing something or if there was a deeper way to reach God's heart. One day, as I poured out my frustrations before Him, a story from the Bible came to mind.

It was Matthew 17:14–21. A desperate father had brought his son, tormented by seizures and a demon, to Jesus' disciples.

But they could not heal him.

When the father turned to Jesus, the boy was instantly delivered.

Later, the disciples, puzzled by their failure, asked Jesus why they couldn't cast out the demon.

Jesus answered them plainly:

"Because of your unbelief; for assuredly, I say to you, if you have faith as a mustard seed, you will say to this mountain, 'Move from here to there,' and it will move; and nothing will be impossible for you".

"However, this kind does not go out except by prayer and fasting."

(Matthew 17:20–21, NKJV)

That last part pierced through my heart, soul, and spirit like a sharp sword;

"<u>by prayer and fasting</u>."

Up until that point, I had prayed with all my might. But I had not combined my prayers with fasting. I decided then that if fasting was the key, I would do it.

So I began another chapter in my spiritual journey, one marked by long days of fasting, intense prayer and endless pleading with God. I fasted often - sometimes for a single day, and at other times for several days.

I denied myself food, water, and comfort, believing that my sacrifice would move the hand of God.

But weeks turned into months.
Months turned into years. And still, my desperate need stood before me, unshaken, unmoved, like a towering mountain.
Each time I finished a fast, I looked for a miracle.

Each time, I faced disappointment.
And yet, I couldn't stop praying.
Prayer pulled me like gravity.
Even in my lowest moments, even when I
decided I would quit, my lips still
whispered, "Lord, please help me."
Over time, the silence began to feel like
rejection.

It twisted into a lie that whispered in the
dark: "God has abandoned you".
That lie grew roots in my mind. I started to
believe it. Depression crept in like a slow
fog. It was during this season that God
reminded me of something I had tried to
bury, my sin.
Quietly, in prayer, He whispered to me:
"You caused this demise."

God reminded me of the ways I had disobeyed Him, the things I had done that dishonored Him.

I felt the weight of it.

The truth is, sometimes we pray for breakthrough and miracles while ignoring the barriers of our own rebellion and disobedience.

In my case, God was peeling back layers I had ignored for years. The words cut me to the core. I realized that in many ways, I had strayed.

I had sinned against God. And while I had been pleading for His intervention, I had not fully dealt with my own repentance.

I broke down completely. Tears streamed down my face as I confessed my sins before Him.

I asked for forgiveness, not just for the mistakes of the past, but for the hardness of my heart – the pride that made me think my fasting and prayers could somehow ignore the past and force God's hand.

Psalm 51:17 states, *"The sacrifice you desire is a broken spirit. You will not reject a broken and repentant heart, O God."* (NLT)

And so, broken, I came before Him.

My fasting became less about begging for my need, and more about humbling myself, seeking His forgiveness, and longing to be restored.

But even after years of fasting, praying, and repenting, God remained silent.

My need stood tall as ever.

Sometimes, I felt things only got worse with each prayer.

And deep inside, exhaustion began to grow.

Discussion Questions:

1. What role has fasting played in your spiritual journey?
2. Do you believe fasting can deepen faith when prayer alone feels unanswered?

Reflection Exercise:

1. Choose one day this week to skip a meal and spend that time in prayer.
2. Write down what you sense God speaking during that fast.

Prayer:

Dear Lord, please help me to seek you wholeheartedly with both prayer and fasting.

Let my hunger for you be greater than my hunger for anything else. Amen.

CHAPTER THREE

BREAKING POINT

I had reached the end of myself.

Years of prayer had changed nothing.

Years of fasting had changed nothing.

Years of waiting seemed useless. I was left staring at the same mountain, taller and stronger than ever.

I was weary, broken, and empty.
Death began to look like the only escape.
It whispered promises of relief, of silence, of rest from the torment. For the first time in my life, the thought of leaving this world felt less terrifying than the idea of continuing to live in it.
But every time I pictured the act of suicide, my children's faces would appear before me.
Every time I pictured their laughter, their questions, and their future without a mother, the image would tear through me like a blade. My heart would sink into my stomach, and uncontrollable tears would follow.
I was trapped in a torment I couldn't explain to anyone. Even my closest family didn't know the depth of my struggle.

To them, I was still "Naomi, the Pastor, the strong and prayerful one."
But inside, I was crumbling.
I had decided to give up on God and give up on life. And yet, I couldn't stop praying. Decades of daily prayer had wired my soul to cry out, even when I no longer wanted to believe. Then it happened.

In the middle of my hopelessness and brokenness, the voice of the Lord broke through the silence. Not in thunder.
Not in fire. The sky did not open.
But in a still, clear and undeniable whisper, God said: *"Naomi, I have pardoned you. I will show you mercy through my grace."*

And then the words of God in **Isaiah 41:10** rang in my spirit:

"Don't be afraid, for I am with you. Don't be discouraged, for I am your God. I will strengthen you and help you. I will hold you up with my victorious right hand."

I froze. Could this really be God?

Could the One I thought had abandoned me actually care enough to be here, speaking, promising, assuring, encouraging and guaranteeing my future?

For the first time in years, a bright light flickered inside me.

Not a flood, just a flicker.

But it was enough to brighten my spirit.

The Lord Himself had become my hope.

And yet, like Gideon in Judges 6, I was unsure.

Was this truly God's voice or just my
desperate mind telling me what I wanted to
hear?
So I prayed for confirmation.
 And God gave it. The very next day, my
older brother who knew nothing of my
struggle sent me an image with a Bible verse
on it. I opened the message, and my heart
nearly stopped. I almost collapsed.

The Bible verse? **Isaiah 41:10**.
Out of all the verses in the Bible, he had sent
me the same scripture God had whispered to
me the night before: **Isaiah 41:10**.
That was no coincidence.
That was my fleece, wet with dew while the
ground stayed dry.
That was God's signature on His promise.

I wept, not in despair this time, but in relief. God had not abandoned me after all.

He had been with me all along. Hope returned in my heart; fragile, but real. When God whispered Isaiah 41:10 into my spirit and confirmed it through my brother, it was like the sun rising after years of stormy nights. I had lived so long in darkness that even a flicker of light felt overwhelming.

But this was no flicker — it was a divine promise. I clung to His words like a drowning person clings to a lifeline. Hope had filled my soul.

Romans 12:12 says, *"Rejoice in our confident hope. Be patient in trouble, and keep on praying"*

Hope was the powerful driving force that gave me the patience and grace to continue praying. For the first time in years, death no longer seemed like my only option. Life did. Because the Lord had spoken, and when He speaks, His words are final and eternal. With this new fire inside me, I went back to fasting and praying with renewed strength. I was sure God was about to answer me, and soon. And then it happened.

About four months later, God gave me a mind-blowing miracle. Not the final answer to my desperate need, but something so powerful that it stunned both me and my husband. It was undeniable. It was real. It was God showing His powerful hand.

It was God reminding me that He was still writing my story.

However, this miracle was not the finish line. It was only the beginning.

Discussion Questions:

1. How do you handle moments when despair seems stronger than faith?
2. What keeps you holding on when you feel abandoned by God?

Reflection Exercise:

1. Write a Journal about a season when despair nearly broke you.
2. Write how God sustained you even if you didn't see it at the time.

Prayer:

Dear Lord, when I am on the edge of despair, please be my lifeline. Remind me that you are near, even when I cannot feel or see you. Amen.

CHAPTER FOUR

HOPE

After the mind-blowing miracle, I was convinced my long-awaited breakthrough was moments away. I prayed with even greater fire, fasted with stronger resolve, and prepared my heart to receive the answer I had begged for all those years.

I expected the next miracle to follow
quickly. But that didn't happen. Instead of
favorable doors opening, one by one they
slammed shut. Every time I thought,
"This is it - this is the moment God will do
it,"
I was met with disappointment.
Each new glimmer of hope seemed to
collapse into heartache and setbacks.
Betrayals cut deep. Conspiracies formed
against me.
Unexpected losses knocked the wind out of
my chest. Physical and spiritual attacks
came back-to-back like crashing waves with
no pause to breathe. My head was spinning
faster than *flash in justice league*.
I couldn't understand what was happening.
It made no sense!

God doesn't mislead His children.

He doesn't trick those who trust in Him.

Why would God give me hope, and then allow so much pain to follow?

One day, in the middle of tears and out of frustration, I cried out with a loud voice: "Father, I gave up on this need.

I gave up on you. But you spoke to me! You promised to help me. So why?

Why are things getting worse instead of better?"

After that prayer, I picked up my Bible and let it fall open. My eyes landed on **Numbers 23:19** (NLT): "*God is not a man, so he does not lie. He is not human, so he does not change his mind. Has he ever spoken and failed to act? Has he ever promised and not carried it through?*"

I stopped breathing for a moment.

The words hit me like fire. God was speaking to me again!

He was telling me, "*Naomi, my dear daughter, my promise still stands. Don't look at the chaos — just look at Me.*"

Still, the delays cut deeper than deep.

In Acts 1, after Judas betrayed Jesus and took his own life, the disciples faced the weight of choosing someone to take his place. Peter explained that the new apostle had to be someone who had been with Jesus from the time of John the Baptist until His ascension, and who could testify to His resurrection. They prayed, sought the Lord's will, and cast lots. The lot fell to Matthias, and he was chosen to be among the twelve. The disciples didn't rely on their own wisdom.

They prayed, trusted, and let God choose.
And God answered. This practice of seeking
the Lord's direction through prayer and lots
is one my family and I have also adopted
over the years. Time and again, God has
guided us in surprising, unmistakable ways.

Not long ago, I put this into practice
again. I needed help in a difficult situation
and had identified five people with the
expertise I needed. I wrote their names on
slips of paper, prayed, and asked the Lord to
show me whom He had chosen.
When I cast lots, one name stood out:
a woman I felt sure God had sent to help me.
I hired her, paid her in full, and signed
documents with her.
But when the time came for her to show up,
she refused. She acted as though she were
doing me a free favor, and when I pressed
her, she simply said, "I can't make it."

She showed no remorse, offered no refund, and left me stranded. I was crushed. Confused. Angry. Broken.

I thought: *Had God misled me?*

I felt like another cruel twist in a story that refused to end. I cried out, "Why, Lord?"

"Why are you silent?"

"Why have you allowed this?"

"What reason could possibly justify another disappointment after all these years?"

My faith, which had soared just months earlier after the mind-blowing miraculous breakthrough, had suddenly dropped to its lowest point.

Isaiah 46:9 *came into my spirit:*

"Remember the things I have done in the past. For I alone am God! I am God, and there is none like me."

I started to remember the miracles, the answered prayers, and the countless times God had shown Himself faithful in the past. While thinking about The Lord's resume in my life, *I remembered Joseph in the Bible.* *(Genesis chapters 37-50)*

Joseph was just seventeen years old when God gave him dreams of greatness. He innocently shared them with his brothers, not realizing jealousy had already poisoned their hearts. They betrayed him, sold him into slavery, and cut him off from his family.

He was sold to Potiphar, an officer of Pharaoh, the king of Egypt. Joseph found favor in Potiphar's household, only to be falsely accused by Potiphar's wife and thrown into prison.

Through it all, Bible says that: *"The Lord was with Joseph."*(Genesis 39:2).

God was still writing his story. Even in prison, God used him to interpret dreams. When Pharoah's cupbearer forgot about Joseph, God allowed two years to pass. Then in God's own time, Pharaoh had a dream that only Joseph could interpret.

Within a day, Joseph went from being prisoner to becoming second-in-command over all Egypt. The dreams God gave him as a boy were finally fulfilled.

His brothers eventually came and bowed low before him, just as God had shown him years before.

Joseph's life reminded me, and let it remind you too, that betrayal, slander, disappointment, false accusations, and delays are all part of God's story for us.

They are chapters in our story, not the conclusion. When I was abandoned by the woman I trusted, I thought God had failed me. But like Joseph, I had to realize that God's pen had not left the page. He was still writing my story.

In Isaiah 7:9, God spoke to King Ahaz during a time of fear and war. He said, *"Unless your faith is firm, I cannot make you stand firm."*

God spoke those same words to me. Despite all His promises and past miracles, I was acting like Ahaz. I was focusing more on the enemy than on God's faithfulness. My faith was wavering badly, and God reminded me. He asked me to *let my faith stand firm, or I will not stand at all.*

When God is writing your story, everyone has a role to play.

And they must play their roles methodically. Some will help you. Some will hurt you. Some will betray you. Some will disappoint you. Some will stab you in the back. But none of them can erase or change what God has planned for you. Joseph's story ended in glory because he never let go of faith. Mine is still being written, and so is yours.

Yes, you will stumble. Yes, you will cry. Yes, you will wonder if God has abandoned you. But if you keep holding on, if you let God keep writing, He will bring your story to the beautiful ending He planned.

Joseph went from the pit, to Potiphar's house, to prison, and finally to the palace.

Your journey may not look exactly like Joseph's story, or mine, but God, who is the Author of our stories, is the Author of yours. And when God publishes your story for the world to see, it will be worth every painful chapter. Hang in there!

Discussion Questions:

1. How has God spoken to you in unexpected ways?
2. What confirmations has He given you during seasons of doubt?

Reflection Exercise:

1. Write down one time you asked God for confirmation and how He answered.
2. If you've never done so, pray now for God to confirm His promises in your life.

Prayer:

Heavenly Father, thank you for speaking to me in ways I cannot ignore. Please help me to recognize your voice above my fears. Amen

CHAPTER FIVE

THE BATTLE INTENSIFIES

I received God's confirmation late in the year. But when God makes a promise, the enemy doesn't just sit back quietly and watch it happen. He fights.

And in my case, the enemy fought hard.

From January through August the following year, it felt like I was living in a war zone. The attacks came like waves with no space to breathe in between.

One attack ended, and another began. Sometimes two or three attacks came simultaneously. The waves of battles were relentless, each one threatening to crash my very existence.

My ministry was targeted. My family came under fire. My body was battered.

At times, it felt like every corner of my life was collapsing. There were numerous emergency room visits, countless hospital admissions, unavoidable surgical procedures, false accusations, slander, betrayal, conspiracies, and many other things. *But I saw something clearly: the enemy was fighting me hard because he knew what was coming.*

Satan knew that if God's promise stood, his plan for my life was over.

He knew that if God fulfills His promise, suicide was no longer an option for me, death was no longer in control of my destiny, and shame was not going to be my portion. Satan knew that my life belonged to God and he had already lost the battle.

So he fought me with all the strength he could muster. He fought me with all the powers and agents of hell.

And though the battles raged, I chose to stand strong and tall with The Lord as my Armor and Shield.

Like Daniel in Daniel chapter 10, whose prayers were heard in heaven on the first day he started fasting and praying, but delayed for twenty one days by the spirit prince of the kingdom of Persia (a spiritual opposition), I learned that my prayers had already been heard in heaven.

And that God's answer was on the way. However, the spiritual warfare was real, the spiritual opposition was fierce, but so was my God's faithfulness.

Satan was trying very hard to block the way as he tried to do to Daniel. But no matter how long it took, no matter how fierce his attacks, I refused to give up on the hope I had found in the Lord. I kept on praying. Even when my body was weak, I prayed.

When my heartfelt numb, I prayed.
When I was too sad to pray, I prayed.
There were days when my prayers were full of strength and fire. There were days when they were broken sighs and hums. There were days when my prayers were repetitive. But I still prayed with my heart and soul.

My prayers still rose to heaven.

Psalm 23 became my anchor: *Verse 1 says,*

"The Lord is my shepherd"

That is my life's motto.

Verse 4 says, *"Yea, though I walk through the valley of the shadow of death, I will fear no evil; For You are with me; Your rod and Your staff, they comfort me."*

The valley I was facing was real. It was not a joke or a movie. The shadows that threatened my future were real. I wasn't imagining them. But so was The Lord, my Shepherd, my Rock, my Refuge, my Shield who was leading the way. And somehow, even in the fire and attacks, I found strength. The enemy was able to bruise me, but he couldn't break me, he couldn't kill me.

My story wasn't in his hands.

My story was in God's hands.

I realized without a doubt that Satan was furious. He knew I had chosen life over death, faith over despair. He knew quitting was no longer an option for me. He knew his time to hold me captive was about to end. So he launched his fiercest attacks to shake me, break me, distract me, and force me to doubt God's word.

But through every attack, God kept bringing me back to His promises.
God kept reminding me of His faithfulness. God kept reassuring me that He was in control. Even on the days when my knees trembled and my legs felt like they wanted to give way, God steadied me with His Word. My hope had been rekindled, but my faith was still being tested in fire.

Discussion Questions:

1. How do you recognize when you are relying on people instead of God?
2. In what ways has God reminded you of His faithfulness during trials?

Reflection Exercise:

1. Reflect on a time when people failed you but God remained faithful.
2. Write it as a testimony to encourage yourself.

Prayer:

Dear Lord, keep me from putting my hope in people more than in you.
Remind me that you alone are faithful and true. Amen.

THIS PAGE INTENTIONALLY LEFT BLANK

CHAPTER SIX

THE BREAKTHROUGH

I remember it like it was yesterday.
It was a hot Sunday morning in Texas.
My children's summer vacation was almost
over, they were returning to school that
Wednesday.
As always, I got up and prepared for church.
I didn't know that day would change
everything.

After the service ended, I took my teenage daughter to Burlington for back-to-school shopping. She picked out a few clothes, and we headed to the fitting room. While waiting for her to try them on, I checked my email out of habit. That's when I saw it. The email.

I recognized the sender immediately.
My heart sank. My pulse raced.
Fear gripped my hands and legs.
"*On a Sunday*?" I asked myself.
I couldn't bring myself to open it - not there, not then, not in front of my daughter.

My daughter peeked out of the fitting room and gave me a look that silently asked, "Mom, are you okay?"

I forced a smile. "I'm fine,"

I told her, urging her to finish quickly.
She chose her favorites, and we paid at checkout.

On the drive home, I tried to steady my breathing. The radio was already tuned to 89.3 KSBJ.

They were playing "Goodness of God" by CeCe Winans.

Tears welled in my eyes as I sang along. All my life you have been faithful…

By the time we reached the house, I couldn't hold it in anymore. I pulled into the garage. I asked my daughter to go inside while I stayed in the car.

Alone, I prayed:

"Father, let your will be done. Give me the strength to accept whatever is in this message."

Then, with trembling hands, I opened the email. And there it was - the notification that God had finally done it. The promise He had whispered to me years ago was now reality. What He had written in heaven, He had published on earth.

I sat in the car, weeping uncontrollably. I found myself on the garage floor, weeping, praising, and thanking God for His faithfulness.

Psalm 126 came alive in me: "*When the Lord brought back His exiles to Jerusalem, **it was like a dream**! We were filled with laughter, and we sang for joy. And the other nations said, 'What amazing things the Lord has done for them.' Yes, the Lord has done amazing things for us! What joy!*"

It was like a dream indeed.

After years of crying, fasting, praying, doubting, and nearly giving up, the Lord proved Himself faithful.

He reminded me that He "*is not a man that He should lie, nor the son of man that He should change His mind*" (Numbers 23:19).

God had kept His word. He did exactly what He said He would do for me. That email was more than good news - it was the signature of God confirming that my story was never abandoned. God Himself had finished what He started.

Discussion Questions:

1. How do you usually respond when God finally answers a long-awaited prayer?
2. What song or scripture reminds you of God's faithfulness?

Reflection Exercise:

1. Create a "testimony playlist" of songs that remind you of God's goodness.

2. Write down one scripture to stand on in future seasons of waiting.

CHAPTER SEVEN

GOD THE AUTHOR

When the long-awaited breakthrough finally came, it felt almost unreal. For years, I had carried the weight of unanswered prayers, endless fasting, and nights filled with tears.

Suddenly, that burden was gone.

God had answered.

Looking back now, I see that my life was never out of God's hands. The long nights of tears, the endless fasting, the unanswered prayers that felt like silence—all of it was a chapter, not the whole story.

What I thought was God's absence was actually His preparation.

What I thought was punishment was actually pruning. God was writing my story.

When I was at the edge of despair, convinced death was my only escape, He wrote mercy and grace into my pages. When Satan hurled his arrows of sickness, betrayal, and fear, God wrote endurance into my soul.

When I thought I had reached the end of my life, He reminded me with Hebrews 12:2, *"I am the Author and the Finisher of your faith."*

I now understand what Romans 5:3–4 means:

"We can rejoice, too, when we run into problems and trials, for we know that they help us develop endurance. And endurance develops strength of character, and character strengthens our confident hope of salvation." (NLT)

Endurance. Character. Hope.

Those are the chapters God was writing while I was crying for quick solutions. And then, one day, the Author turned the page.

That email was not just an answered prayer it was proof that God never leaves a story unfinished.

Just as He brought the Israelites back from exile, just as He rescued Daniel after the prince of Persia tried to block his answer, just as He made Joseph the Governor of Egypt even though Joseph's brothers had planned slavery for him, just as He gave Hannah a son after years of tears and prayers, just as He turned an orphan into a Queen, just as He raised Jesus on the third day, He also completed what He started in me.

Beloved, I want you to hear this:

God is still writing your story too. Maybe you are where I once was, surrounded by impossible needs, exhausted from praying, tempted to give up. Maybe you feel like God has abandoned you. But I stand as a witness to tell you that He is not finished with you. Your tears are not wasted. Your prayers are not ignored. Your fasting is not in vain.

Even the silence is a sentence in His manuscript. One day, the page will turn in your favor.

The very thing you thought would break you will become the testimony that strengthens you. The Red Sea will part. The walls of Jericho will fall. The barren land will blossom.

And when it happens, you will say just as I did: "*It was like a dream*! The Lord has done amazing things" for me. (Psalm 126:1–3)

God is the true Author. He alone holds the pen. And He has promised in Jeremiah 29:11: "*I know the plans I have for you," says the Lord. "They are plans for good and not for disaster, to give you a future and a hope.*"

The Author is still writing. My story continues. So does yours. And in His time, He will publish your manuscript too. If you are in a season of waiting, don't give up. The same God who wrote my story is writing yours. Hold on. Pray, fast, and stay faithful, even when it feels like the heavens are silent. One day, you too will say: IT WAS LIKE A DREAM.

Discussion Questions:

1. How has suffering shaped your character and endurance?
2. Can you recall a time when trials pushed you closer to God rather than away from Him?

Reflection Exercise:

1. Write a Journal about a battle you faced and how it shaped your faith.
2. Then write a declaration of endurance you can speak over your life.

Prayer:

Dear Lord, let every trial refine me instead of breaking me. Give me the endurance to keep standing until my breakthrough comes. In Jesus' Name I pray. Amen.

CHAPTER EIGHT

REFLECTIONS AND LESSONS

Looking back, I realize that God could have answered my prayer in a moment, but instead, He chose to walk with me through years of waiting, fasting, tears, and trials.

Because He was not just answering my prayer, He was transforming me.

My desperate need became the very tool He used to shape my faith, break my pride, teach me perseverance, and draw me closer to His heart.

Lessons learned

1. **Prayer must become your life – Nonnegotiable**:

Philippians 4:6 says, "*Don't worry about anything; instead, pray about everything. Tell God what you need, and thank him for all he has done*" (NLT)

For many years, prayer became the air I breathed. At times it felt as though my prayers went unanswered, but in truth, every prayer was being woven into God's magnificent plan.

Prayer kept me alive when despair whispered death, disgrace, and shame.

Prayer kept me connected to God even when I thought He was silent.

2. **Fasting is mandatory – never optional**:

Fasting is the Spiritual key that unlocks the Power of God and neutralizes Satan's Power.

When Jesus told His disciples in Matthew 17:21 that, "*This kind does not go out except by prayer and fasting,*" (NKJV)

He was revealing an important spiritual key. Fasting is not a way to twist God's arm, it is a way to align our spirit with His will.

Through fasting, my flesh weakened but my spirit grew stronger.

Fasting can be hard, but it makes all the difference.

3. **Repentance Brings Restoration**:

2 Chronicles 7:14 says, "*if my people who are called by my name will humble themselves and pray and seek my face and turn from their wicked ways, I will hear from heaven and will forgive their sins and restore their land.*"

God reminded me of my sins, and I realized that part of my delay was connected to the need for repentance. True breakthrough doesn't come from demanding answers from God, it comes from humbling ourselves before Him.

4. **God's Timing is Perfect**:

I was looking for an immediate answer. I wanted my need met yesterday. But God is not bound by my time clock. He works according to His timetable, and His timing is always perfect. What felt like a delay was actually preparation for me, for my family, for my ministry, and for the testimony He was writing through me.

5. **God Confirms His Word**:

Just as He confirmed His promise to Gideon with the fleece in Judges 6:36–40, God confirmed His word to me again and again - through my brother, through scripture, through circumstances. When we ask sincerely, God never leaves us confused. His voice will always align with His Word.

6. **Delay does not mean "No"**:

The hardest part of my journey was waiting. But as Daniel's story in Daniel chapter 10 shows us, sometimes our prayers are answered immediately in heaven, but the manifestation is delayed due to spiritual opposition and spiritual warefare (Ephesians 6:10–18).

My waiting wasn't wasted; it was a season of preparation.

7. **Enemies <u>Can</u> Be a Blessing**:

The attacks, betrayals, and disappointments that the enemy used to break me were actually the tools God used to strengthen me. Without those trials, I might never have developed the endurance, character, and hope described in Romans 5:3–4.

My enemies pushed me deeper into prayer. They pushed me closer to God. They forced me to never let go of my faith. For that, I am strangely, oddly, and uniquely grateful.

8. **God's Promises Never Fail**:

Numbers 23:19 became my anchor: *"God is not a man, so he does not lie. He is not human, so he does not change his mind. Has he ever spoken*

and failed to act? Has he ever
promised and not carried it through?"

I learned that even when
circumstances scream otherwise,
God's Word still stands firm.

9. **Hope Is Stronger Than Death**:

There were moments I thought death was the only escape for me. But God's mercy pulled me back.

He reminded me in Isaiah 41:10 that He would strengthen me and help me, and hold me up with His victorious right hand.

Hope in God became stronger than despair, stronger than fear, stronger than death.

This journey was never just about receiving my need. It was about becoming the woman God created me to be.

My testimony is proof that no matter how dark it gets, no matter how long it takes God is faithful.

10. **The true meaning of "whom you know":**

The adage "*whom you know*" means that your victory and success hinges on your professional and personal network connections. Some even say, "*It's not what you know, but whom you know*"

"***Whom you know***" is the world's way of teaching us to depend on connections such as friends, family, colleagues, neighbors, and acquaintances, to navigate success by the people we know in high places. And there's some truth in that.

It is undeniable that "*whom you know*" can propel you forward in many situations, but it is also extremely fleeting and very fragile. Because people **can** disappoint, people **can** let you down, people **can** betray you when you least expect it.

Sometimes we place our hope in someone with influence, trusting they will step in to help.

But when they don't, whether because they wouldn't, couldn't, or just didn't see our need as a priority, the weight of that disappointment can be crushing.

Relying on people can make you vulnerable because people are unpredictable.

It is true that doors do open through networks and influence.

But what happens when those doors slam shut in your face when you need them the most?
What happens when the very people you trust are the ones who betray you? What happens when the people you depend on fail to come through for you?

I have been taught to respect people in high places ever since I was a child.
I saw others strive to sit at the feet of influential men and women, hoping their fate would be rewritten through human favor. Some succeeded.
Many were disappointed. Others betrayed.

I have lived long enough to see what happens when your hopes are anchored in fallible people. They promise you rain and leave you parched. They say you'll rise and watch you fall. Their intentions may be good, but their intentions don't write your destiny, only God does.

Bible tells us in Psalm 20:7-8, "*Some trust in chariots, and some in horses; But we will remember the name of the Lord our God. They have bowed down and fallen; But we have risen and stand upright.*" (NKJV)

This is the very foundation of divine trust: remembering the name of the Lord when everything else fails.

When we place our hope solely in *"whom we know*," we risk placing our destiny in the hands of imperfect people. In doing so, we essentially hand the pen of our lives to someone unequipped to write it. That is a dangerous thing to do.

There is only One qualified to author your story and mine; He is the One who knew you and sanctified you before you were formed in your mother's womb (Jeremiah 1:5, NKJV).

The only qualified author is The One who has plans not to harm you but to prosper you, to give you a future and a hope (Jeremiah 29:11). The only qualified author is the One who knows what will happen tomorrow, and can do something about it.

Discussion Questions:

1. Have you ever relied on someone you know in a position of influence, hoping they would help, but things didn't turn out the way you expected?
2. Have you ever trusted someone to write your story only to be disappointed?
3. How did you deal with the disappointment?
4. Can you identify areas in your life where you've yet to trust God with the pen?
5. How do you recognize when you are relying on people instead of God?
6. In what ways has God reminded you of His faithfulness during trials?

Reflection Exercise:

1. Reflect on a time when people failed you but God remained faithful.

2. Write it as a testimony to encourage yourself.

Prayer:

O Lord my God, I confess that I have often tried to control the narrative of my life or handed the pen over to other people who could never write it well.

Today, I fully surrender my story into your hands. Write it beautifully, purposefully, and divinely. Please increase my faith in you.
In Jesus' Name I pray.
Amen.

CHAPTER NINE

YOUR PAST DOESN'T DISQUALIFY YOU

Our past does not disqualify us and our limitations do not limit the power of God.

Romans 8:28, "*And we know that all things work together for good to those who love God, to those who are the called according to His purpose.*" (NKJV)

When we look at the life of Paul (who was formerly known as Saul), we see a man who was passionately opposing the gospel of Jesus Christ. He persecuted Christians, dragged them into prison, and stood in agreement with their deaths. Yet one encounter with Jesus Christ changed everything for him (Acts 9).

Not only did Jesus forgive Paul, he was also called to be an apostle. He was entrusted with spreading the very gospel he once tried to destroy.

I can imagine how overwhelming and surreal it must have been for him to realize that God had turned his past into a testimony of grace. It probably felt like a dream when he realized that Jesus was writing his story all along.

Esther was an orphan who was raised by her uncle Mordecai. Her family had no royal background or influence.

When Mordecai encouraged her to join in the beauty pageant for the king's search for a queen, it must have felt unlikely that she would be chosen.

Because not only was Esther an orphan, she was "a commoner". But that didn't matter to God. Her past wasn't a requirement for God to elevate her. God qualified her even though her past disqualified her.

She obeyed Mordecai's words, and God granted her favor by making her queen.

I imagine Queen Esther must have thought she was dreaming. God can do anything!

Later, it was her position as Queen that allowed her to intercede and save her people from destruction (Esther 4:14).

Both Paul and Esther remind me that **God is writing my story and yours, even when we cannot see the ending.**

As I mentioned earlier, our past does not disqualify us, and our limitations do not limit the power of God.

What seems ordinary, destroyed, or broken can become the very chapter God uses for His glory. Again, God can do anything!

Both Paul and Esther were part of something much larger than themselves.

Paul spread the gospel across the world while Esther preserved God's chosen people as Queen. Neither of them could see the full picture, but they both trusted God's leadership.

Beloved, Esther went from Orphan to Queen.

Paul went from enemy of the gospel to Apostle of Jesus Christ. You may not see the end of your story right now, but God is weaving your story into His greater plan. Like Paul and Esther, you are part of something much larger and greater than yourself. Just trust God with every single chapter of your life.

Discussion Questions:

1. Think about the parts of your life that feel wasted, broken, or insignificant.

2. Could it be that God is weaving them into a bigger story? Just like Paul's past and Esther's humble beginnings, your story is not over. God is the Author, and He never wastes a chapter. Let Him continue writing your story.

3. Do you believe God can do anything?

4. What past mistake or failure makes you feel unqualified?

5. In what ways does 2 Corinthians 5:17 transform your understanding of your past?

6. Which biblical character's story encourages you most, and why?

7. What steps can you take to live more fully in your new identity in Christ?

8. How might God use your past to help others?

Reflection Exercise:

1. Make a list of regrets or mistakes you feel hold you back.
2. Pray through each one, surrendering them to God.
3. When the enemy whispers, "you're disqualified," declare God's Word (Romans 8:1, 2 Corinthians 5:17).
4. Your past can be a powerful encouragement to someone else struggling with shame.
5. Share your testimony.
6. Ask God daily, "How can I serve you today with the life you've redeemed?"

Prayer:

Heavenly Father, thank you for being the Author of my story. Please help me to trust that even my past, my weaknesses, my flaws, and my limitations are in your hands. Teach me to walk in faith, like Paul who embraced your calling, and like Esther who stepped into her royal divine assignment.

May my life reflect your glory and serve your purpose. Please give me the grace to live a life that is holy, pleasing, and acceptable unto Thee. I pray this in The Mighty Name of Jesus Christ, Amen.

CHAPTER TEN

LIVING IN VICTORY

When the promise was finally fulfilled, it felt like I had crossed through fire and come out refined, not burned.

The very thing that once brought me shame, fear, and sorrow had become my testimony.

I realized something important: the fulfillment of God's promise is not the end of my story. It is the beginning of a new chapter in my life and ministry.

For years, my life was marked by waiting, crying, and fighting battles I didn't think I could survive. Now, my days are marked by gratitude, faith, peace, and praise. The same God who carried me through the valley is the same God who now leads me beside still waters.

Victory Changed My Perspective:

• I no longer see God as distant or silent. I know Him as a Father who hears, who sees, and who answers in His perfect time.

• I no longer ask "Why me?" Instead, I ask "What is God teaching me?" Every battle is an opportunity for deeper faith.

• I no longer see waiting as wasted time. Waiting is training. Waiting is shaping. Waiting is proof that God is preparing something greater than I could imagine.

When I see people going through what I went through; depression, hopelessness, unanswered prayers, I can look them in the eye and say, "I know how it feels.

But I also know how it ends."

My life has become living proof of Isaiah 61:3: *"To all who mourn in Israel, he will give a crown of beauty for ashes, a joyous blessing instead of mourning, festive praise instead of despair."*

Receiving the promise wasn't just for me. It was so I could give glory to God and encourage others to hold on. Out of the ten lepers Jesus healed in Luke 17:11-19, only one of them returned to thank Jesus.

I refuse to be ungrateful like the other nine. Every chance I get, I will testify that God is faithful. I will continue to tell the world that God can be trusted. Victory doesn't mean life is now free of challenges, problems, and trials.

New battles will come, but my heart is anchored in God's past faithfulness. If He could carry me through that storm, He will carry me through every storm ahead.

I wake up each day knowing I am living proof of Psalm 126:5, *"Those who plant in tears will harvest with shouts of joy."*

I planted in tears for years. Now I am harvesting *"with shouts of joy"* to the glory of God.

Discussion Questions:

1. What areas of life do you struggle to live victoriously?
2. How does knowing Jesus has already overcome change the way you face battles?
3. Which "armor of God" (Ephesians 6) do you need to strengthen in your daily walk?
4. How can you encourage others to live in victory through your testimony?

Reflection Exercise:

1. **Pray daily in victory:** Start each day thanking God for triumph in Christ.
2. **Guard your mind:** Replace negative thoughts with God's promises (Philippians 4:8).
3. **Stand on Scripture:** Memorize victory verses (Romans 8:37, 1 Corinthians 15:57).

4. **Walk in obedience:** Victory is experienced when we follow God's leading step by step.
5. **Encourage others:** Share testimonies of God's power at work in your life.

CHAPTER ELEVEN

A WORD FOR YOU

Beloved, if you are reading my story,
I know you may be in your own
season of waiting, pain, or confusion.
Maybe you've prayed for years,
fasted until your strength ran out, and
still the mountain hasn't moved.

Maybe you feel like God has gone silent. Maybe, like me, you've been tempted to give up on life itself.

Please know that God has not forgotten about you. The same God who remembered me will remember you. The same God who turned my tears into laughter is the same God who will dry your tears.

1. **Don't Stop Praying**:

Even when it feels pointless, keep praying. Prayer is not just about getting answers, it is about staying connected to the One who holds all the answers. Daniel prayed and fasted for 21 days before the angel broke through with his answer. Your breakthrough may already be on the way. So don't give up now.

2. **Don't Stop Believing in God**:

Matthew 17:20, Jesus promises that *"if you had faith even as small as a mustard seed, you could say to this mountain, 'Move from here to there,' and it would move. Nothing would be impossible"*

Hold on to that small mustard seed. God can plant it, water it, grow it, and use it to uproot the huge mountain in front of you.

3. **Don't Stop Waiting**:

Habakkuk 2:3 says, *"This vision is for a future time. It describes the end, and it will be fulfilled. If it seems slow in coming, wait patiently, for it will surely take place. It will not be delayed."*

Waiting doesn't mean God is ignoring
you. Waiting means God is preparing
you and preparing the blessings He
has for you. Waiting means your
miracle is on the way.

4. **Don't Stop Trusting God's word**:

When your heart screams "Why God?"
Trust Him anyway.
When your strength is gone, lean on Him.
When you don't see the way, remember that
He is the Way.
Keep trusting God's leadership.

5. **Hold On to His Promises**:

As I have mentioned a few times in this
book, Numbers 23:19 says that God is not a
man that He should lie. If He has spoken, He
will bring it to pass.

A time comes in every Christian's life when their story takes a turn they never saw coming. A time comes when things don't align with the dreams, the prophecies, or the promises spoken over their life.

This is the page that tempts many of us to give up and stop trusting God - the Author. But this is also the moment that should strengthen our faith to hold on tightly to the Author of our lives.

Joseph's rise to power was not a reward, it was a responsibility. The same God who kept him in the pit, who favored him in prison, now positioned him in the palace. This wasn't about revenge. It wasn't even about Joseph. It was about God's purpose to preserve a nation.

Many of us want God to write a beautiful story, but we want to be the main character.

But in God's narrative, He is the hero.
We are the vessel.
And when we truly surrender the pen, we begin to see that every twist and trial was never random, it was sacred and intentional.
God does not make mistakes.
God's stories do not follow the world's narratives. His qualifications transcend the expectations of the world.
In His story, the least becomes the greatest. The forgotten becomes the favored. And the rejected one becomes the redeemer of generations.

I often wonder about the tears Joseph must have cried the night before Pharaoh called him. I wonder if he thought God had abandoned him. I visualize the silence in his cell when the cup-bearer forgot his promise.

I imagine one day, out of nowhere, the prison guards come. Open his cell door. And everything changes instantly.

Beloved, picture it; this is how God works. He makes all things beautiful in His perfect time. God had been preparing Joseph for this moment. And God is preparing you for something majestic.

Discussion Questions:

1. Have you surrendered the pen of your story to God, or are you still editing His work?

2. What part of your life currently doesn't make sense but might be sacred preparation?

3. How can you shift your focus from being the main character to being a willing vessel?

Reflection Exercises:

1. Tell God that He is the potter and you are the clay (Jeremiah 18:1-6). Ask Him to mold and shape you for His glory.
2. Surrender your heart, mind, soul and spirit to God.
3. Release full control of your life to Him.

Prayer:

Heavenly Father, today I surrender my desire for control. I choose to let you be the Author and the Hero of my life. Please help me steward what you've placed in my hands, and teach me to trust you when the story takes an unexpected turn. I yield my future to your design.

Do with me as you see fit.
In Jesus' Name I pray. Amen.

Your story is not over.
Your breakthrough may be one prayer away,
one act of faith away, one fast away, or one
sunrise away.
Hang on to God.
He will not fail you.

My Final Prayer for You

O God of mercy and compassion, lifter of men, way maker, miracle worker, my Savior, my Fortress, my Redeemer, my Provider, my Protector, and my Shepherd, I lift up every person holding this book, every weary soul, every broken heart, every desperate cry to you.
Please remind them that you are near.
Strengthen their faith in you.
Let them see your hand moving even in the silence.
Bring them to their own Psalm 126 moment, where their mouths will be filled with laughter and their tongues with songs of joy.
Make your ears attentive to their prayers.
In The Mighty Name of Jesus Christ I pray, Amen.

THIS PAGE IS INTENTIONALLY LEFT BLANK

CHAPTER TWELVE

CONCLUSION
THE PUBLISHED STORY

"Looking unto Jesus, the author and finisher of our faith, who for the joy that was set before Him endured the cross, despising the shame, and has sat down at the right hand of the throne of God."

-    Hebrews 12:2 NKJV   -

My journey has taught me two unshakable truths: God is faithful. He does not lie. He does not abandon His children. Even when it feels like heaven is silent, He is still writing your story. For many years, I thought my unanswered prayers meant God had forgotten me. But now I know He was shaping me, stretching my faith, and preparing a testimony that would glorify His name. What I once thought was my destruction turned out to be my deliverance.

Looking back, I realize every delay had a purpose. Every unanswered prayer shaped my faith. Every trial drew me closer to God. And when the breakthrough came, it wasn't just about the answered prayer it was about the transformation in me.

My story is now in your hands, not to glorify my endurance, but to glorify God's faithfulness. Truly, when the Lord restored my life, ***it was like a dream.***

I stand today as living proof that prayer works, that fasting strengthens, that repentance restores, and that hope in God never disappoints.

If my story has reached your hands, it is because God wanted you to know that you are next. Your miracle is on the way.

Discussion Questions:

1. What lesson from this story speaks most to your own season of waiting?
2. How can you encourage others with your testimony while still waiting for your own breakthrough?

Reflection Exercise:

1. Write a letter to your future self about what you are waiting on God for today. Seal it, and open it when your breakthrough comes.

Final Reflection and Prayer:

1. What impossible situation are you facing right now?

2. Are you willing to keep trusting God even when answers seem delayed?

Prayer of Thanksgiving

Heavenly Father, I thank you because you are faithful. Even when I don't see the answers, I know you are working.
Strengthen my heart to wait on you.
Keep me from despair and help me to trust your timing.
Fill me with joy when my miracle comes, so I too may say; *It was like a dream.*
In The Mighty Name of Jesus Christ I Pray, Amen.

EPILOGUE

ALL GLORY BELONGS TO GOD

When I look back at the sleepless nights, the tears, the depression, and the times I almost gave up, I can only lift my hands and say: "Glory be to God!"

God turned my mourning into dancing. He replaced my despair with hope. He proved Himself as my Shepherd, my Deliverer, my Savior, my Master, my Way Maker, my Miracle Worker, and my Redeemer.

I dedicate this testimony not to my own endurance but to the grace and mercy of God who held me when I was falling, who lifted me when I was sinking, and who loved me when I felt unlovable.

Beloved, as you close this book, may you open a new chapter in your own life filled with unshakable faith, undeniable miracles, a prayerful life, and unending joy.

Psalm 126:3 says, *"The Lord has done great things for us, and we are filled with joy."* Amen!

CLOSING PRAYER

Heavenly Father,

I seal this book and every reader under your love and protection. May the testimonies shared here stir faith, birth courage, and release hope.

Let every heart be reminded that you are the God who restores, the One who turns mourning into dancing, and the Keeper of every promise.

May we live our days trusting you fully until our own "dream" moments arrive.

In the Mighty Name of Jesus Christ I pray, Amen.

PRAY THIS PRAYER

Lord God of Heaven's Armies,

I come before you with all my pain, fears, and needs. There are times when I feel forgotten, but today I choose to believe that you see me and you hear me. You are my Shepherd, my Helper, and my Deliverer. Please don't leave me.

Heavenly Father, please strengthen my faith when I am weak. Give me hope when I feel hopeless and useless. Please remind me that your promises never fail. I surrender my situation into your mighty hands. I trust you to write my story, and I believe you will make all things beautiful in your own time.

Thank you, Lord God Almighty, for your unfailing love, for hearing me, and for never leaving me. I ask you this in the Mighty Name of Jesus Christ! Amen.

APPENDIX

G R O U P   S T U D Y   G U I D E

This Group Study Guide is designed to make *It was like a dream* a resource for deeper reflection, discussion, and encouragement, whether read alone, with family, or in a small group.

Chapter 1: Desperate Need

Scripture Reading:

Psalm 31:14-15, *"But I am trusting you, O Lord, saying, "You are my God!" My future is in your hands. Rescue me from those who hunt me down relentlessly."* (NLT)

Mark 14:36, *"Abba, Father,"* he cried out, *"everything is possible for you. Please take this cup of suffering away from me. Yet I want your will to be done, not mine."* (NLT)

Discussion Questions:

1. Have you ever faced a situation that seemed impossible to overcome?

2. How did you respond when it seemed like God was silent?

Reflection Exercise:

1. Write down one situation in your life that feels like the Red Sea - impossible to cross.

2. Then write a prayer of trust, asking God to make a way.

Chapter 2: Add Fasting

Scripture Reading:

Mathew 17:14-21, "*And when they had come to the multitude, a man came to Him, kneeling down to Him and saying, [15] "Lord, have mercy on my son, for he is an epileptic and suffers severely; for he often falls into the fire and often into the water. [16] So I brought him to Your disciples, but they could not cure him.*"

[17] Then Jesus answered and said, "O faithless and perverse generation, how long shall I be with you? How long shall I bear with you? Bring him here to Me." [18] And Jesus rebuked the demon, and it came out of him; and the child was cured from that very hour.

[19] Then the disciples came to Jesus privately and said, "Why could we not cast it out?"

*[20] So Jesus said to them, "Because of your unbelief; for assuredly, I say to you, if you have faith as a mustard seed, you will say to this mountain, 'Move from here to there,' and it will move; and nothing will be impossible for you. [21] **However, this kind does not go out except by prayer and fasting**."* (NKJV)

Discussion Questions:

1. What role has fasting played in your spiritual journey?

2. Do you believe fasting can deepen faith when prayer alone feels unanswered?

Reflection Exercise:

1. Choose one day this week to skip a meal and spend that time in prayer.

2. If possible, try two, three, or seven days fasting and seek The Lord in prayer.

3. Write down what you sense God speaking during that fast.

4. Record the results in a journal.

Chapter 3: Breaking Point

Scripture Reading:

Isaiah 41:10, *"Fear not, for I am with you; Be not dismayed, for I am your God. I will strengthen you, Yes, I will help you, I will uphold you with My righteous right hand"* (NKJV)

2 Corinthians 4:8-9, "We are hard-pressed on every side, yet not crushed; we are perplexed, but not in despair; persecuted, but not forsaken; struck down, but not destroyed" (NKJV)

Discussion Questions:

1. How do you handle moments when despair seems stronger than faith?

2. What keeps you holding on when you feel abandoned by God?

Reflection Exercise:

1. Journal about a season when despair nearly broke you.

2. Write how God sustained you even if you didn't see it at the time.

Chapter 4: Hope

Scripture Reading:

Isaiah 40:31, *"But those who wait on the Lord Shall renew their strength; They shall mount up with wings like eagles, They shall run and not be weary, They shall walk and not faint."* (NKJV)

Hebrews 11:1, *"Now faith is the substance of things hoped for, the evidence of things not seen."* (NKJV)

Discussion Questions:

1. How has God spoken to you in unexpected ways?

2. What confirmations has He given you during seasons of doubt?

Reflection Exercise:

1. Write down one time you asked God for confirmation and how He answered.

2. If you've never done so, pray now for God to confirm His promises in your life.

Chapter 5: The Battle Intensifies

Scripture Reading:

1 Samuel 17:47, *"Then all this assembly shall know that the Lord does not save with sword and spear; for the battle is the Lord's, and He will give you into our hands"* (NKJV)

Exodus 14:13-14, *"And Moses said to the people, "Do not be afraid. Stand still, and see the salvation of the Lord, which He will accomplish for you today. For the Egyptians whom you see today, you shall see again no more forever. The Lord will fight for you, and you shall hold your peace."* (NKJV)

Discussion Questions:

1. How do you recognize when you are relying on people instead of God?

2. In what ways has God reminded you of His faithfulness during trials?

Reflection Exercise:

1. Reflect on a time when people failed you but God remained faithful.

2. Write it as a testimony to encourage yourself.

Chapter 6: The Breakthrough

Scripture Reading:

Acts 16:25–26, *"But at midnight Paul and Silas were praying and singing hymns to God, and the prisoners were listening to them. Suddenly there was a great earthquake, so that the foundations of the prison were shaken; and immediately all the doors were opened and everyone's chains were loosed."* (NKJV)

Micah 2:13, *"The one who breaks open will come up before them; They will break out, Pass through the gate, And go out by it; Their king will pass before them, With the Lord at their head."* (NKJV)

Discussion Questions:

1. How do you usually respond when God finally answers a long-awaited prayer?

2. What song or scripture reminds you of God's faithfulness?

Reflection Exercise:

1. Create a "victory playlist" of songs that remind you of God's goodness.

2. Write down one scripture to stand on in future seasons of waiting.

Chapter 7: God The Author

Scripture Reading:

Hebrews 12:2, *"looking unto Jesus, the author and finisher of our faith, who for the joy that was set before Him endured the cross, despising the shame, and has sat down at the right hand of the throne of God."* (NKJV)

Philippians 1:6, *"being confident of this very thing, that He who has begun a good work in you will complete it until the day of Jesus Christ"* (NKJV)

Psalm 139:16, *"Your eyes saw my substance, being yet unformed. And in Your book they all were written, The days fashioned for me, When as yet there were none of them."* (NKJV)

Discussion Questions:

1. How has suffering shaped your character and endurance?

2. Can you recall a time when trials pushed you closer to God rather than away from Him?

Reflection Exercise:

1. Journal about a battle you faced and how it shaped your faith. Then write a declaration of endurance you can speak over your life.

Chapter 8: Reflections and Lessons

Scripture Reading:

Psalm 118:8, "*It is better to trust in the Lord Than to put confidence in man.*" (NKJV)

2 Timothy 2:13, "*If we are faithless, He remains faithful; He cannot deny Himself.*" (NKJV)

Deuteronomy 31:6, "*Be strong and of good courage, do not fear nor be afraid of them; for the Lord your God, He is the One who goes with you. He will not leave you nor forsake you.*" (NKJV)

Hebrews 13:8, "*Jesus Christ is the same yesterday, today, and forever.*" (NKJV)

Discussion Questions:

1. Have you ever trusted someone to write your story only to be disappointed?

2. What emotions surfaced when they let you down?

3. Can you identify areas in your life where you've yet to trust God with the pen?

4. How do you recognize when you are relying on people instead of God?

5. How can past disappointments help you develop a stronger faith in God?

6. In what ways has God reminded you of His faithfulness during trials?

7. Why is it dangerous to place ultimate trust in people rather than God?

Reflection Exercise:

1. Reflect on a time when people failed you but God remained faithful.

2. Write it as a testimony to encourage yourself.

Remember: Appreciate people, but depend on God alone.

Chapter 9: Your Past Does Not Disqualify You

Scripture Reading:

2 Corinthians 5:17, "*If anyone is in Christ, he is a new creation. The old has passed away; behold, the new has come.*"(NKJV)

Psalm 103:12, "*As far as the east is from the west, so far does He remove our transgressions from us.*"(NKJV)

Discussion Questions:

1. What past mistake or failure makes you feel unqualified?

2. How does 2 Corinthians 5:17 change your perspective on your past?

3. Which biblical character's story encourages you most, and why?

4. What steps can you take to live more fully in your new identity in Christ?

5. How might God use your past to help others?

Reflection Exercise:

1. Write it down: Make a list of regrets or mistakes you feel hold you back.

2. Pray through each one, surrendering them to God.

3. When the enemy whispers "you're disqualified," declare God's Word (Romans 8:1, 2 Corinthians 5:17).

4. Your past can be a powerful encouragement to someone else struggling with shame. Share your testimony.

5. Ask God daily, "How can I serve You today with the life you've redeemed?"

Chapter 10: Living In Victory

Scripture Reading:

2 Chronicles 20:15, *"Do not be afraid nor dismayed because of this great multitude, for the battle is not yours, but God's."* (NKJV)

1 Corinthians 15:57, *"But thanks be to God, who gives us the victory through our Lord Jesus Christ."* (NKJV)

Romans 8:37, *"Yet in all these things we are more than conquerors through Him who loved us."* (NKJV)

Discussion Questions:

1. What areas of life do you struggle to live victoriously?

2. How does knowing Jesus has already overcome change the way you face battles?

3. Which "armor of God" (Ephesians 6) do you need to strengthen in your daily walk?

4. How can you encourage others to live in victory through your testimony?

Reflection Exercise:

1. Pray daily in victory: Start each day thanking God for triumph in Christ.

2. Guard your mind: Replace negative thoughts with God's promises (Philippians 4:8).

3. Stand on Scripture: Memorize victory verses (Romans 8:37, 1 Corinthians 15:57).

4. Victory is experienced when we follow God's leading step by step.

5. Share testimonies of God's power at work in your life.

Chapter 11: A word for you

Scripture Reading:

1 Thessalonians 5:16–18, *"Rejoice always, pray without ceasing, in everything give thanks; for this is the will of God in Christ Jesus for you."* (NKJV)

James 5:16, *"Confess your trespasses to one another, and pray for one another, that you may be healed. The effective, fervent prayer of a righteous man avails much."* (NKJV)

Persevere In Prayer

1. Jesus (Luke 22:39–44) – Prayed earnestly in Gethsemane before the cross.

2. Daniel (Daniel 6:10) – Prayed faithfully even when threatened with death.

3. Hannah (1 Samuel 1:9–20) – She prayed for years before God gave her Samuel.

Discussion Questions:

1. When have you been tempted to give up on prayer?

2. Which Bible character's example of persistent prayer inspires you most?

3. How does Luke 18:1 encourage you to keep praying?

4. What specific need in your life requires continued prayer today?

Reflection Exercise:

1. Have you surrendered the pen of your story to God, or are you still editing His work?

2. What part of your life currently doesn't make sense but might be sacred preparation?

3. How can you shift your focus from being the main character to being a willing vessel?

4. Choose times daily; morning, afternoon, and night, to connect with God. Set a prayer schedule.

5. Write your prayer requests and note when God answers in a prayer journal.

6. Pray the word of God. Declare promises from God's Word in your prayers.

7. Place sticky notes or phone reminders to keep prayer at the center of your day.

8. Join a prayer partner or prayer group for encouragement. Pray with others. Corporate prayer is important.

Conclusion: The Published Story

Scripture Reading:

1 John 5:14–15, *"Now this is the confidence that we have in Him, that if we ask anything according to His will, He hears us. 15 And if we know that He hears us, whatever we ask, we know that we have the petitions that we have asked of Him."* (NKJV)

Discussion Questions:

1. What lesson from this story speaks most to your own season of waiting?

2. How can you encourage others with your testimony while still waiting for your own breakthrough?

Reflection Exercise:

1. Write a letter to your future self about what you are waiting on God for today.

2. Seal it, and open it when your breakthrough comes.

AUTHOR'S NOTE

Writing this book has been one of the most humbling and faith-stretching journeys of my life. I did not set out to write a story for others. I was simply trying to survive the waiting, the prayers, and the tears.

But as God began to move, I realized He was not just answering me; He was crafting a testimony meant to be shared.

I pray you do not just see my struggles and victories on these pages, but that you also recognize your own story reflected here. If you are waiting, you are not alone.

If you are weary, take courage. If you are rejoicing, give thanks loudly, for your testimony will encourage others.

This book is my offering back to God and my invitation to you: keep walking, keep trusting, keep on believing, and don't give up.

Jehovah Nissi, Addonai, Jehovah Jireh, Yahweh,

Lord God of Heaven's Armies, The Living God of Abraham, Isaac, and Jacob, and The God of Naomi, who made my story *IT WAS LIKE A DREAM* is the same God who is writing yours.

He will publish your manuscript in His time.

Remember God's resume in your life and hold on tightly to Him in faith.

With love and Blessings,
 - Rev. Mrs. Naomi Antwi

ABOUT THE AUTHOR

Rev. Mrs. Naomi Antwi stands as a beacon of faith, leadership, and empowerment in the Christian community. With a life dedicated to the service of God and humanity, she has seamlessly woven her roles as a Minister of the Gospel, an Author, a wife, a mother, and a Pastor into a tapestry of extraordinary dedication and impact.

Rev. Mrs. Naomi Antwi serves as the Pastor at Spiritual Enrichment Church, where she leads with unparalleled devotion and vision. Her sermons are known for their depth, inspiration, and the profound ability to connect biblical teachings to the everyday lives of her congregation. Under her leadership, Spiritual Enrichment Church thrives on spiritual growth, unity, and outreach.

Her pastoral care extends beyond the pulpit, as she is deeply involved in mentoring and guiding members of her community through the vicissitudes of life.

As an Author, Rev. Antwi has penned numerous works that reflect her theological insights and experiences. Her writings are a source of inspiration and education for many, offering wisdom, encouragement, and practical guidance for living a life rooted in faith. Through her books, she reaches a global audience, touching lives far beyond the walls of her church.

In her personal life, Rev. Antwi is a devoted wife and mother. Her family is the bedrock of her strength and a testament to her ability to balance her demanding ministerial responsibilities with her roles at home.

She often shares her experiences and lessons from family life, providing a relatable and heartfelt perspective that resonates with many.

In addition to her pastoral duties, Rev. Antwi is the visionary founder and President of the Women Ministers United Fellowship.

This organization is a haven for female pastors, first ladies, and female ministers, offering them a platform for Spiritual and physical support, growth, and collaboration.

Through this fellowship, she champions the cause of women in ministry, advocating for their empowerment and providing them with the resources and networks necessary to thrive in their callings.

Rev. Mrs. Naomi Antwi also serves as the Treasurer of the Ghanaian Ministers Fellowship-USA.

Rev. Antwi's influence extends beyond her immediate community.

Her vision is rooted in a deep commitment to spiritual enrichment, social justice, and community development. She tirelessly works to create environments where individuals can grow in their faith, find their purpose, and make a positive difference in the world. Rev. Antwi embodies the principles of dedication, compassion, and leadership.

Her multifaceted role as a Minister, Author, Wife, Mother, Founder, and President reflects a life lived in service to God and others. Through her ministry and initiatives, she continues to inspire and uplift countless individuals, leaving an indelible mark on the community and beyond. Her journey is a testament to the power of faith, resilience, and unwavering commitment to the calling she has embraced with grace and fervor.

A CALL TO ACTION

If this book has spoken to you, I would love to hear your story. Share your testimony with others - whether in your church, your family, your friends, your community, or even directly with me.

Your breakthrough can encourage someone else who is still waiting.

You can connect with me at:
Email: revnantwi@gmail.com

Website: www.naomiantwi.com

All Social Media Platforms:

@revnaomiantwi

Together, let's keep spreading hope and faith so that more voices can one day say:

"When I allowed God to finish, *IT WAS LIKE A DREAM*" MAY GOD BLESS YOU"

R e a d e r   F e e d b a c k

Your voice matters. If this book has encouraged you, I invite you to leave a review on Amazon, Goodreads, or wherever you purchased your copy.

Reviews help other readers discover the message of hope and faith in *It was Like A Dream*.

Even a few sentences about how this book touched your life can make a difference.

If you'd like, you can also share your reflections directly with me. I love hearing testimonies of how God is moving in people's lives.

Thank you!

Connect with the Author

I would love to stay in touch with you beyond these pages. Whether you have a testimony to share, a prayer request, or simply want to say hello, please reach out:

Email: revnantwi@gmail.com

Website: www.naomiantwi.com

All Social Media Platforms: @revnaomiantwi

Let's continue encouraging one another in faith so that many more can one day say *It was like a dream*.

MORE BOOKS BY THE AUTHOR

GRAB YOUR COPY